T0023658

WHAT IF YOU WERE ON THE PACIFIC FRONT IN WORLD WAR II?

AN INTERACTIVE HISTORY ADVENTURE

by Lisa M. Bolt Simons

CAPSTONE PRESS
a capstone imprint

Published by You Choose, an imprint of Capstone
1710 Roe Crest Drive, North Mankato, Minnesota 56003
capstonepub.com

Library of Congress Cataloging-in-Publication Data
Names: Doeden, Matt, author.
Title: What if you were on the Pacific front in World War II? : an interactive
history adventure / by Matt Doeden Other titles: What if you were on the Pacific
front in World War Two?
Description: North Mankato, Minesota: You Choose, an imprint of Capstone,
[2023] | Series: You choose: World War II frontlines | Includes bibliographical
references. | Audience: Ages 8-12 | Audience: Grades 4-6 | Summary: "The
Japanese and their invading forces have wreaked havoc across eastern Asia. They've
even attacked the U.S. Naval Base Pearl Harbor. You're part of the Allied Forces
helping defend the Pacific Front. YOU CHOOSE how you will help fight for
freedom on the high seas? Will you make the right decisions to help forward your
cause and come home safe?"— Provided by publisher.
Identifiers: LCCN 2022041595 (print) | LCCN 2022041596 (ebook) | ISBN
9781666390872 (hardcover) | ISBN 9781666390865 (paperback) | ISBN
9781666391022 (pdf)
Subjects: LCSH: World War, 1939-1945—Campaigns—Pacific Area—Juvenile
literature. | Plot-your-own stories.
Classification: LCC D767 .D537 2023 (print) | LCC D767 (ebook) | DDC
940.54/26—dc23/eng/20220830
LC record available at https://lccn.loc.gov/2022041595
LC ebook record available at https://lccn.loc.gov/2022041596

Editorial Credits
Editor: Mandy Robbins; Designer: Hilary Wacholz; Media Researcher: Jo Miller;
Production Specialist: Tori Abraham

Image Credits
Alamy: Military Collection, 29, Pictorial Press Ltd, 46, PJF Military Collection, 19,
Sueddeutsche Zeitung Photo, 55; Associated Press: AP Photo, 75; Getty Images:
Hulton Archive, Cover (background), 1, Interim Archives/U.S. Navy, 4; Library of
Congress, 14; Naval History & Heritage Command: NARA, 87, 94, NARA/U.S.
Navy, 26, 36, 99, NARA/U.S. Navy photo by Photographer 2nd Class William G.
Roy, 58; Shutterstock: Volina, 106, Wicked Digital, 77; Wikimedia: NARA, 11,
NARA/U.S. Navy, 22, 60, National Museum of the U.S. Navy, Cover (Marines)

Design Elements
Shutterstock: Roman Amanov

TABLE OF CONTENTS

Pearl Harbor, Hawaii, before the Japanese attack

ABOUT YOUR ADVENTURE

YOU are on the front lines of World War II
(1939–1945). In the Pacific, the Allied forces are
fighting to stop the Japanese from taking control
of the islands in the Pacific Ocean. War planes
fill the skies. Ships and submarines speed through
the sea. Battles rage on shore. Can you help the
Allies win the war? YOU CHOOSE which paths
to take. Your choices will guide the story. Live
or die. Succeed or fail. It's up to you to help the
Allied forces claim victory.

• Turn the page to begin your adventure.

CHAPTER 1

WAR IN THE PACIFIC

Europe has been embroiled in battle for years. Adolf Hitler rose to power in Germany in 1933, with plans to take over all of Europe. In 1939, Hitler's army invaded Poland. Soon, many other countries had joined the war. Germany, Italy, and Japan were called the Axis powers. The Allied powers included Great Britain, France, and Canada.

U.S. President Franklin Roosevelt has tried to keep your country out of war. But on December 7, 1941, Japan attacks Pearl Harbor in Hawaii. War has come to the United States.

Furious, the United States joins the Allied effort. You're ready to fight for your country. Japan is trying to rule the Pacific. Your goals are to defeat the Japanese and survive. Will you succeed?

- To defend the attack on Pearl Harbor, turn to page 8.
- To join the Battle of Midway at sea, turn to page 38.
- To battle the Japanese on Guadalcanal, turn to page 72.

CHAPTER 2

THE JAPANESE ATTACK PEARL HARBOR

It's Sunday, December 7, at almost 8:00 a.m. You're stationed at Pearl Harbor to help with operations in the Pacific. It has been a peaceful experience so far. But suddenly, sounds of explosions break the silence. You hear the rumble of planes overhead.

You're shocked. The war's in Europe! How did it get to beautiful Pearl Harbor, Hawaii? With a sick feeling, you realize you're under attack!

- To be on board the USS *West Virginia*, go to page 9.
- To be on board the USS *Solace*, turn to page 25.

You're the head cook on the USS *West Virginia*. You're cleaning up after breakfast when an explosion rocks the ship. Plates shatter. Silverware clatters to the floor. Huge metal pots get thrown off the stove. You drop the dishes and grab hold of the washbasin. The alarm blares.

"John! Moses!" you yell at the other cooks. "You all right?"

"Yes, sir!"

You three are the only Black men on the ship. You're not allowed to serve in combat positions. But this is an emergency situation. You must help.

"I'm heading on deck!" you tell them. You rush out of the galley and up the stairs.

Turn the page.

The sky is thick with Japanese planes dropping torpedoes into the water. The weapons head straight into the ships and explode!

Other planes head over the mainland and drop bombs. Just then, a plane flies overhead, and it drops a bomb on the *West Virginia*. You brace yourself as the ship rocks again!

You scan the harbor. Fire and smoke rise from the seven battleships docked there. But there are more than 100 ships in the harbor. You hear screams as the explosions continue.

Your ship has been hit twice. It's already tilting in the water. Do you stay and defend a sinking ship? Or should you defend the airfield and airplanes on Ford Island? If the Japanese were to destroy them, it could set back the Pacific operations for the U.S. for months.

- To stay on the ship, go to page 11.
- To head to Ford Island, turn to page 19.

You decide to stay on board. You may be able to help your fellow sailors—there are more than 1,000—defend the *West Virginia*.

Just then, a sailor yells, "Incoming!" A bomb blasts the ship. You sprint up to the bridge to see how you can help.

The Japanese attack on Pearl Harbor

Turn the page.

Captain Bennion is slumped over the ship's wheel. A sailor is sitting up, leaning against the wall. His uniform is bloodstained.

"What happened?" you ask as you rush to the captain. He's still breathing.

"Shrapnel flew in and hit us," the sailor says weakly.

You gently heave the captain over your shoulder and head to the stairs. You set him on the landing.

Another hit! You know the *West Virginia* is strong. It's built with steel for battles. But how much more can it take before it's at the bottom of the harbor? You run back to the bridge and pick up the sailor in your arms. He's dead. You put his body by the captain.

You could get the wounded across to the USS *Tennessee*. Or you could stay and defend the ship. You haven't been trained in using antiaircraft guns, but you may just have to learn by doing.

- To help the wounded, turn to page 14.
- To defend the ship, turn to page 17.

There's no way this ship is going to make it. And if the ship goes down, so does everyone on board. You haven't been trained in using a weapon, but you are a former football player, and you are strong. The gunners can shoot down the planes while you focus on moving the wounded to the *Tennessee*.

You run to the deck to look for sailors who are injured but awake. You step carefully. The oil that's spilled from the explosions has made the deck slippery. The thick black smoke makes it difficult to see and breathe. You come across another sailor checking bodies too.

"We can make quick work if we do this together!" you yell.

"You got it!" he yells back.

The two of you move to a sailor with a broken ankle. Together, you carry him to the side of the *West Virginia* nearest the *Tennessee*. You throw a rope to a sailor on the other ship. He ties it to the railing. You pick up the injured sailor, and he grabs the rope.

"Hand over hand all the way across!" you instruct him.

Turn the page.

Just as you turn to another sailor to put him on the rope, you hear whistling. Your brave deeds are cut short. Another bomb explodes into the *West Virginia*'s deck. You don't survive. You will be among the 2,402 other victims of the attack.

THE END

To follow another path, turn to page 7.

To learn more about the Pacific front, turn to page 103.

If you can stop the planes, you stop the attacks. You run to the gunnery, do your best to aim at the planes, and pull the trigger. You're surprised at the kickback, as the gun slams against your shoulder with each rapid shot. But you hold steady.

Three Japanese pilots make a sharp turn back toward the ship, and all drop torpedoes. Two miss the ship's hull, but the other meets its mark. You're knocked off your feet. You jump up again.

"Come on!" you yell, firing off more shots. You hit two planes, but this is no time to celebrate. You keep firing.

Moments later, an officer finds you.

"Abandon ship!" he commands.

Turn the page.

You don't want to stop fighting, but the ship has taken on too much damage. You and the remaining sailors escape on lifeboats and watch as fireboats try to put out the flames. Before long, the *West Virginia* sinks, taking many men to a watery grave.

THE END

To follow another path, turn to page 7.
To learn more about the Pacific front, turn to page 103.

There's no way the *West Virginia* is going to make it. It's been hit two times—the ship shakes and shudders—now three. The blast slams your body against the wall, and you fall to the floor. You shake your head as you stand. You can't hear well.

The USS *Nevada* in flames during the Japanese attack

Turn the page.

You'll be able to help defend Pearl Harbor better on land. Machine guns on Ford Island won't sink like antiaircraft weapons on the ship. You'll also be able to defend the airfield. Airplanes are vital in war.

Ford Island has a Navy base with a repair shipyard, submarine base, barracks, and hospital. It also has weapons and ammunition storage. You want to head there. But how? You could swim. But the water is slick with spilled oil and full of debris. Or you could take a rope from the *West Virginia* deck across to the USS *Tennessee*. You could hop on the floating catwalk from there to the Ford Island beach. But you're not sure how much damage the *Tennessee* has taken.

- To swim to Ford Island, go to page 21.
- To run for the catwalk, turn to page 24.

Running might be faster, but you're a good swimmer. Plus, the water offers some protection from the bombs and torpedoes. You run to the side of the ship, climb over the railing, and jump. Just in time. Another hit!

Not too far from you, thick black oil fills the once clear water. Flames dance upon it. Even the water is on fire. You swim in the other direction, past pieces of ship wreckage and bodies. Your heart breaks. Then you come across one sailor who's alive! He's on his back kicking. His hands on his chest are burned black.

"Let me help!" you exclaim.

He doesn't reply.

Turn the page.

You swim in front of him and wrap
one arm around his chest. Your other arm
paddles the two of you between massive
battleships. Suddenly, an explosion rocks the
USS *Oklahoma*. Pieces of the ship fall to the
water. One chunk heads right toward you.
You duck. It smacks into the water behind you.

Finally, you reach the shore of Ford Island. Explosions are everywhere. Bullets pepper the ground as you run for the hospital. People are running all over the place. You stop a nurse.

"I found this sailor in the water," you tell her. She looks at his hands and leads the sailor away.

You run out of the hospital. The Japanese planes are gone. You look around in shock. Airplanes are destroyed. Buildings are burning. Fires and smoke cover the island. You can't imagine what the rest of Pearl Harbor looks like.

You're amazed and thankful that you're alive but wish you could've done more. You have a feeling more battles will come. The president is sure to declare war now. You hope to take part in the effort.

THE END

To follow another path, turn to page 7.
To learn more about the Pacific front, turn to page 103.

Taking a rope to the *Tennessee* will be faster. The floating catwalk will then take you to the Ford Island shore. You step carefully on the slick, oily deck to reach the side of the *West Virginia*. You wave down a sailor on the *Tennessee*. You throw him a rope, and he ties it to the railing. You climb over the railing and start inching across the rope, hand over hand, toward the *Tennessee*. You make it!

The *Tennessee* doesn't have nearly as much damage as your ship. You run to the other side and head down to the floating catwalk that leads to the shore. You're almost there when a downed Japanese bomber falls from the sky straight toward you. Your last thought before you're hit is that you should've stayed with your ship.

THE END

To follow another path, turn to page 7.
To learn more about the Pacific front, turn to page 103.

The morning of December 7, you are sleeping soundly when something jolts you awake. Gunfire and explosions shake your bed.

"COMMAND BATTLE STATIONS!" barks a voice over the speaker system.

You're a nurse aboard the hospital ship the USS *Solace*. It is your first station since completing training. You jump out of bed. You hear people running up to the deck. Peering out your porthole, you see smoke rising from the USS *Oklahoma*.

You look to the sky. It's filled with Japanese planes. They're dropping torpedoes into the water and bombs on ships! There are fires everywhere, even on Ford Island. It's the heart of the harbor. There are barracks, weapons, and ammunition there. It's where ships are repaired. Worse yet, there's a hospital on Ford Island. Fellow nurses are over there!

Turn the page.

As you look out the window, a bomb hits the USS *Arizona*. A huge explosion shakes the *Solace* again. Your hand covers your mouth before you snap out of your shock.

The USS *Arizona* starting to sink

You force yourself to stop looking out the window and get dressed quickly. You slam your room door and pin on your cap as you rush to the surgical unit. Critically injured patients will be arriving any second. Even before you get there, you think about the supplies you need to prepare: the morphine, the tannic acid for burns, the plasma, the instruments, the bandages.

Your fellow nurses, Teresa and Sally, are already there when you arrive. Together, you prepare the stations.

Soon, the medics start bringing in the victims—badly wounded men rescued from the water. Many are burned, some have been hit by shrapnel, and others have broken bones. Some are moaning in pain. Others stay silent. You quickly assess who is in the worst condition.

Turn the page.

"This one here," you bark, pointing at one bed. "He goes to the burn unit. Quickly!"

All of a sudden, your skirt is grabbed from behind.

"I don't want to die!" a sailor moans.

He is hanging on to your uniform for dear life. He has shrapnel wounds everywhere and is covered in oil. Gently, you take his hand.

"You're going to be okay," you tell him over the chaos in the room.

"Please don't leave me," he begs.

It's not possible to stay with him with so many patients, and more are coming. You need to get back to work. But how can you leave this terrified sailor?

There's a good chance he won't make it much longer. Should you get back to work or stay and comfort him in his last moments?

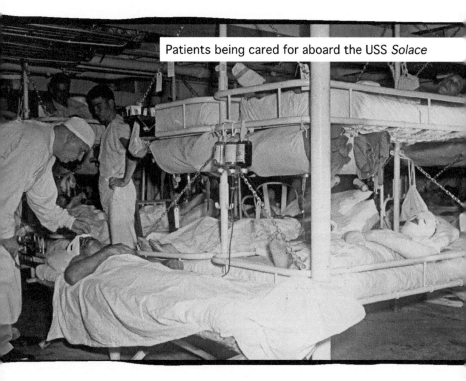

Patients being cared for aboard the USS *Solace*

- To get back to the patients, turn to page 30.
- To stay with the patient, turn to page 32.

You must get to the other patients as quickly as you can.

"What's your name?" you ask the sailor. You look on one of the prep tables and search for a morphine syringe. Morphine will help him with the pain and put him to sleep. But the table is in shambles. Everything you, Teresa, and Sally laid out is a bloody, oily mess. Your hands desperately search the table.

"Stanley," the sailor replies.

You found it.

"Stanley, I'm going to give you something for the pain, okay?"

"Okay."

You squeeze his hand and then give him the shot in his arm.

"Don't leave me."

"I'll be right back," you assure him.

You run to help with several more patients. A few minutes later, you turn back to Stanley. He's gone. Perhaps you should have comforted Stanley in his last moments. The guilt of leaving him haunts you.

THE END

To follow another path, turn to page 7.
To learn more about the Pacific front, turn to page 103.

More victims come in, but you just can't leave this kid. He's terrified.

"What's your name?" you ask.

"Stanley."

"Nice to meet you, Stanley."

He doesn't smile. "I can't feel my left side," he gasps, panicked.

Your heart sinks. That's a symptom of internal bleeding. He doesn't have much time left.

You hear a loud scream of agony across the room. Dr. Haakenson calls out, "I need assistance over here!"

Stanley looks at you with panic in his eyes.

"I won't leave you, Stanley. Where are you from?"

"Iowa," he replies.

"I've never been there," you say. "Tell me about it."

For a few minutes, Stanley describes the farm he grew up on. You ask him about his family. His voice trails off as he talks about his mother. It's not long before he's gone. You know you did the right thing staying with him in his final moments. But still, your heart sinks.

Again, Dr. Haakenson cries out, "I need some help over here now!"

You run to the doctor. He stands over another sailor blackened with oil and burns with a leg that's shredded to pieces. You pull up a screen for privacy and assist the doctor with an amputation. You've never witnessed this kind of surgery before. You thought you had a strong stomach, but this pushes you over the edge.

Turn the page.

You pull back the curtain. Everywhere you look you see wailing, injured sailors. You're overwhelmed by this brutal reality. You know you should keep working, but you're not sure you can.

- To keep working despite feeling sick and overwhelmed, go to page 35.

- To take a quick breather, turn to page 37.

Too many sailors need help. You can't leave no matter how you feel.

"You've been trained for this," you tell yourself.

But training on plastic dummies and practicing giving shots to a banana did not train you for this. This is war. War is horrible.

You hurry to help Sally. She's working on a sailor with a burnt shoulder and two broken fingers. You apply ointment to his burn.

"You look paler than your uniform," Sally says.

"I'm fine," you lie.

"Step outside for one minute," Sally says.

"I'll be all right," you say.

Turn the page.

the USS *Solace*

Just then, a bomb hits close. The *Solace* shakes. Already queasy, you're thrown to the floor. You hear and feel several of your bones breaking.

You end up a patient instead of caretaker. You spend the rest of the day in a bunk, wishing you could help others. You hope you can heal quickly and get back to duty as soon as possible. You know this war isn't over.

THE END

To follow another path, turn to page 7.
To learn more about the Pacific front, turn to page 103.

You tell Sally that you need a quick breather. The blood, the screams, the burns, the death . . . it's overwhelming you. You run to the toilet and throw up. Afterward, you wash your face and rinse your mouth. You feel a little better.

You return to the surgical unit and keep treating the injured and dying men and women crowding the hospital ship. You spend the rest of the day there. By evening, you and the rest of the medical staff on board have cared for more than 130 patients.

THE END

To follow another path, turn to page 7.
To learn more about the Pacific front, turn to page 103.

CHAPTER 3

THE UNITED STATES FIGHTS BACK AT MIDWAY

It's 1942, and the world is at war. You're part of the United States military. Even though you're not in direct combat, your job impacts what happens during the war.

Currently, your focus is the Midway Islands, an area 1,100 miles northwest of Hawaii. Midway is a threat to Japan because a U.S. Naval Air Station sits there. It houses 4,000 American servicemen. Military B-17 bombers and PBY Catalina aircraft are also there, ready to accept orders to fight the Japanese.

Since the Pearl Harbor attack, the Americans have been battling the Japanese over possession of the Pacific. Japan wants to rid the entire area of the United States and control all of it. This strategy would help Japan gain more territory.

It's only a matter of time before the Japanese strike again. You know they want control of the base and the airfield at Midway. The American military can't let this happen. It will take teamwork for your side to win the Battle of Midway. Cryptanalysts will decode messages intercepted from the Japanese. Photographers will document combat scenes as they happen in real time.

- To be a cryptanalyst, turn to page 40.
- To be a photographer, turn to page 57.

"Sir!" one of your translators says. "Check this message we decoded!"

You rush to his desk and read it. The Japanese are talking about attacking Midway!

"Are there more messages coming through?" you ask.

"Yes, sir!"

It's May 1942. You and your team are in Pearl Harbor. You're the officer in charge of the Combat Intelligence Unit, or Station HYPO.

Your team's job is to listen to Japanese messages coming over the radio. They are also encoded, or scrambled, but you've cracked the code. Your team calls this code JN-25. As messages come through, you and your team unscramble and then translate the messages into English.

You feel responsible for the attack on Pearl Harbor. At the end of 1941, your team could only read parts of the Japanese code. Your boss, the intelligence officer in Washington, D.C., lost trust in you. You can't let your country down again.

You scan the message. Four aircraft carriers will be used in the Midway attack. Four? The Japanese must be planning to knock out the American forces.

Who do you relay this sensitive information to? Your boss in Washington? The Navy department you work for is there. That would be the proper chain of command, the official process in the Navy. Or should you inform Lieutenant Commander Edwin Layton? You two spent three years together in Japan. He's the intelligence officer for Admiral Nimitz, the commander in chief of the U.S. Pacific fleet at Pearl Harbor.

Turn the page.

You're giving Layton daily reports, anyway. Breaking the chain of command could damage your career but saving hundreds or even thousands of American lives would be worth it. And you doubt your boss in Washington would have faith that your information is accurate. How do you move forward?

- To follow the chain of command, go to page 43.
- To break the chain of command, turn to page 45.

You're in the Navy. You have to follow the chain of command and relay the information to your boss, Captain Redman, in Washington, D.C. He's part of the Inter-department Communication Liaison Division in the Office of the Chief of Naval Operations. Your team has cracked the latest code. You hope your boss believes you.

You walk to headquarters and place a call to Redman. The operator puts you through.

"You have news?" Redman asks.

"Midway will be attacked," you say.

There is silence on the other end.

"Captain Redman?" you ask.

"Our team believes the Japanese will target the West Coast."

Turn the page.

"They're wrong," you argue. "Everything my team is reading here—"

"I'm telling you it's the West Coast." His voice doesn't waver. "Good day." Redman hangs up on you.

Could your information be wrong? After all, he's also getting intelligence from other Navy sources. Should you return to the office and double check what your team found? Or do you call him back and try to convince him you're correct?

- To return to the office to review the messages, turn to page 48.

- To call him back, turn to page 50.

You're friends with Lt. Commander Layton. You need to tell him what you know. Although part of you feels bad for breaking the chain of command, it's your duty to put the lives of American sailors first.

You jog to Layton's office.

"Edwin, we need to talk." You stand at his desk, catching your breath. "My team discovered the next target. It's Midway."

"You sure?" he asks, excited.

"Yes."

"I believe you. I just need to convince Nimitz," he says.

Turn the page.

But Admiral Nimitz tells Layton that he needs verification that your information is true. Nimitz says the intelligence department in D.C. sent him a telegram stating the attack will be on the West Coast.

Admiral Nimitz

Do you step back and let Nimitz and your boss, Captain Redman, decide which direction to take? You're sure Redman will eventually get the Midway messages. Or do you try to prove to everyone that you're right about Midway? American lives are on the line.

- To step back, turn to page 52.
- To prove you're right about Midway, turn to page 53.

Redman works in the Inter-department Communication Liaison Division in the Office of the Chief of Naval Operations. He's stationed in Washington, D.C. Since he's telling you something different, maybe your team is wrong. You go back to your office and review all the messages.

Later, Lt. Commander Layton stops by for the daily progress.

"I thought we had a lead," you begin. "But I called D.C., and Redman said we were wrong."

"Do you think you're wrong?" Layton asks.

You shrug. "Now I don't know."

"Get back to me if you find something else," he says and leaves.

For the next several weeks, you and your team try to verify when and where the next Japanese attack will be. But the Japanese go silent, just like they did before Pearl Harbor. You don't get further orders from Redman except to keep doing what you're doing. What else can you do but follow orders?

When Midway does get attacked in early June 1942, you're crushed. Once again, you feel you failed your country.

THE END

To follow another path, turn to page 7.
To learn more about the Pacific front, turn to page 103.

You and your team spent years figuring out JN-25. After that, decrypting and translating the newest Japanese messages took months. You decide to call Redman back to convince him you're right.

Once again, the operator connects you. Redman finally picks up.

"Please don't hang up," you say. "I have more information. There will be four aircraft carriers. We also know the date and time."

"I'm supposed to believe this after you completely missed Pearl Harbor?" he retorts.

"We didn't have JN-25 figured out then," you explain.

"I'm not hearing Midway from other sources," Redman argues. "I need further verification. Until then, don't share this information with anyone." Again, he hangs up.

You follow Redman's orders. Layton comes to your office weeks later.

"Where have you been?" you ask.

"Busy with Admiral Nimitz preparing for our next counterattack."

"Midway?"

Layton stares at you, baffled. "No, Malibu on the West Coast."

You learn that most of the military forces are now moved to the West Coast. You feel sick. The next day, Japan attacks Midway. Again, you feel you've failed your country.

THE END

To follow another path, turn to page 7.
To learn more about the Pacific front, turn to page 103.

Nimitz is the commander in chief of the entire U.S. Pacific fleet. If he thinks the intelligence Captain Redman is getting in D.C. is correct, you have to let it go. But you're convinced you got it right. You take pride in your job as a cryptanalyst. But your hands are tied when high-powered, higher-ranking people make the decisions.

Unfortunately, several weeks later, the verification comes when the Japanese attack Midway. You're devastated. You should've done more to verify Midway was the target. Now territory, airfields, and lives are lost because you didn't have more nerve to stand up for you and your team.

THE END

To follow another path, turn to page 7.
To learn more about the Pacific front, turn to page 103.

You know you're right. You have to prove it.

The Japanese have been intercepting your messages too. You send a fake message to a U.S. submarine. The message is: *Midway is running out of fresh water.*

Two days later, a Japanese message comes through. Once decrypted and translated, it reads: *AF is running out of water.*

You dash to Layton's office. "This is it!"

You hand him the message.

"'AF' means what?" he asks.

You smile. "Midway."

Layton instructs you to keep reading more messages to get more details of the attack. In the next few days, you collect the information.

Turn the page.

When you bring it to Layton, he suggests telling Nimitz yourself. The two of you go to the admiral's office.

"It's all right here, Admiral," you say. "Midway and the specifics."

"Well done," he says.

You walk back to your office with a spring in your step. You may have just saved thousands of lives. Then you worry. Redman won't be happy to find out you've gone over his head.

A week later, you're called to Nimitz's office.

"I appreciate your work, but you should've told Redman first. He's reassigning you to D.C."

Your heart sinks.

You leave Hawaii days later.

You're in Washington, D.C., when you hear about Midway on the radio. On June 3, the U.S. attacks a few enemy ships. The next morning, Japan attacks Midway. But torpedo bombers from the aircraft carriers USS *Yorktown*, USS *Enterprise*, and USS *Hornet* make a surprise attack on the Japanese fleet. All four of their aircraft carriers are either damaged or destroyed.

a Japanese cruiser at the Battle of Midway

Turn the page.

The next day, the U.S. sinks a Japanese enemy cruiser and damages other ships. The Japanese suffer tremendous losses in the Pacific. And it's all because of you!

Unfortunately, Redman takes credit for decrypting and translating the messages about Midway. You're proud of your work but disappointed too. It is many years before anyone knows how you helped Admiral Nimitz plan and win the surprise attack.

THE END

To follow another path, turn to page 7.
To learn more about the Pacific front, turn to page 103.

You're a photographer stationed on the aircraft carrier USS *Yorktown*, and the Japanese are fast approaching! You grab your camera from your bunk. It's June 4, 1942. Today will go down in history.

You joined the Navy to take photos and shoot video for the Naval Aviation Photographic Unit. "Photograph everything," is the motto. It's your job to get photos and video to the Navy to recruit pilots. They are competing for men with the Army Air Corps. The Navy has to fill 30,000 spots.

Where is the best place to film? Should you run up to the signal bridge? This location would allow you to see in every direction.

Turn the page.

Or should you head to the left, or port, side of the flight deck by a gun crew? Enemy planes would come right at you, but you'd have the protection of the gun crew. Both are dangerous. But both will get you amazing shots.

The deck of the USS *Yorktown* at the Battle of Midway

- To run up to the signal bridge, go to page 59.
- To sprint to the port side, turn to page 67.

You decide to run up to the signal bridge to see all the action. You put your camera strap around your neck, hold the camera tight, and sprint up several flights of stairs. Then you climb a ladder to the highest deck, or crow's nest.

You catch your breath as the American bombers prepare to take off from the *Yorktown*. You snap photos of the sleek airplanes, the pilots checking their instruments, and the catapult officers, or shooters, directing the planes.

One by one, the airplanes head for the skies to find the Japanese. Fighters from the USS *Enterprise* and the USS *Hornet* are in the sky too. You hope they can fend off the Japanese before they reach your ship.

Turn the page.

the USS *Enterprise*

But before too long, Japanese planes fly toward the *Yorktown*. The gunners on the ship engage in antiaircraft fire. You continue to snap photos as the battle heats up.

Suddenly, you're nervous. You feel like a target up here. This view is amazing. But maybe you'd be safer on a lower deck.

- To keep taking photographs on the signal bridge, go to page 61.
- To head down to a lower deck, turn to page 66.

This is where the action is. You're scared, but your job is to get these photos.

All of a sudden, a sailor yells, "Incoming!"

You try to snap a photo of the bomb falling, but it's too fast. It slams into the flight deck! You grab the railing as the ship shakes. You don't want to fall from up here! Another bomb hits! You hold the railing even tighter. You cough from all the smoke. Then a third bomb hits!

When the ship stops shaking, you keep taking photos. Sailors scramble to repair the 12-foot hole in the flight deck and put out fires. Medics help the wounded. Soon, the flight deck is up and running again. Airplanes take off, but more Japanese attack.

Turn the page.

You realize these enemy planes are about to launch long black torpedoes. These weapons will drop in the water and head straight for the ship's hull. The damage could be catastrophic.

Do you photograph the torpedo attack or head to a safer place? Three bombs have already ripped into the ship. Will the ship make it if torpedoes hit? Maybe you should find the closest lifeboat.

- To photograph this attack, go to page 63.
- To head for safety, turn to page 65.

You stay and continue taking photographs. The Navy wants everything documented.

When the Japanese bomber releases the torpedo, the black weapon dives into the water. When the torpedo hits, the *Yorktown* shudders. You grab the railing. The ship tilts to the port side. You don't think the *Yorktown* will make it.

A second torpedo strikes, and the ship tilts even more. The power goes out.

Worse yet, a submarine fires two more torpedoes into the ship's hull. The explosions shake you to your bones. The ship is going down. It's just a question of when.

Captain Buckmaster yells in his megaphone, "Prepare to abandon ship!"

Turn the page.

You look down from your perch and see no safe way to get to the deck. The stairs you ran up have been terribly damaged. Jumping to the deck would surely kill you. Your only chance is to wait for the ship to go down and jump into the water. A lifeboat can pick you up. But you forget one thing—when the ship goes under, it sucks you down with it. Your body sinks to the bottom of the ocean. Your camera footage is lost.

THE END

To follow another path, turn to page 7.
To learn more about the Pacific front, turn to page 103.

No one will see your photos if you go down with the ship. You scramble down the ladder and stairs.

You get down just in time to hear Captain Buckmaster shout into his megaphone, "Prepare to abandon ship!"

The sailors make last-ditch efforts to put out fires and collect necessary Navy equipment. Then they load into the lifeboats. You move as quickly and carefully as you can with your camera equipment. You're relieved when you're safe in the lifeboat. Hopefully, your footage of this devastating battle will inspire more Americans to fight in the Navy.

THE END

To follow another path, turn to page 7.
To learn more about the Pacific front, turn to page 103.

You're growing more nervous. You feel like a target on top of a pole at the tallest point on the ship. How will you help the Navy recruit new pilots if you're not alive to take action photos? You snap a couple more photos of the sailors working hard on the flight deck.

You climb down the ladder and hurry down the stairs. You don't want to go on the flight deck because it's harder to see what's coming. You head to the port side of the ship, instead. Just as you get there, you hear, "Incoming!"

The bomb rips a 12-foot hole in the deck, taking with it the lives of many brave sailors, including your own. The Naval Aviation Photographic Unit will be recruiting new pilots without you.

THE END

To follow another path, turn to page 7.
To learn more about the Pacific front, turn to page 103.

You sprint toward the port side. The enemy will aim at the gun crew, so your photos will be incredible. You hope the gunners protect you.

The American fighters take off from the *Yorktown*. You film them and snap photos of the sailors watching them.

You sit with the gun crew, your stomach in knots. You hope the counterattack keeps the Japanese planes away. You take photos of the flight deck crew and the choppy sea while you wait.

"Do you think the guys got 'em all?" one of the gunners asks.

"Hope so," another replies.

All hopes are dashed when you hear the rumble of planes overhead. You aim your camera.

Turn the page.

Three Japanese bombers head straight toward the *Yorktown*. The gunners at all stations engage in antiaircraft fire. It's so loud!

Then a second bomb hits. The ship shudders, and you hear a grunt and a thud. You turn to see one of the gunners down. Shrapnel from the bomb struck him.

"Get over here and help me!" the other gunner yells.

You're a photographer. You shoot a camera, not a gun! Do you put down the camera and help defend the ship or find another sailor to help the gunner out?

- To defend the ship with the other gunner, go to page 69.
- To find someone else to help the gunner, turn to page 70.

You set down your camera and get behind an antiaircraft gun. It's not what the Navy assigned you to do, but defending your country is the right thing to do. You aim toward the sky and shoot. The third Japanese bomber heads closer to the *Yorktown*.

The scene is hectic. Sailors try to put out fires and repair the bombed deck. Medics help the injured. You and other gunners shoot at the Japanese plane.

You hit the plane, but it still drops its bomb. Its machine guns aim at you too. You're hit before the bomb slams into the deck. Like so many others, you give your life for your country.

THE END

To follow another path, turn to page 7.
To learn more about the Pacific front, turn to page 103.

You've never been trained to shoot anything but a camera. You'll find someone else to help the gunner.

The deck is in chaos with sailors trying to repair the bomb damage and put out fires. You grab the nearest man.

"That gunner!" you yell and point. "He needs help now!"

The sailor runs to the open spot and aims at the Japanese plane heading toward the *Yorktown*.

You get back to taking action shots—sailors trying to save the ship, medics trying to save injured sailors. You glance back at the gunners just in time to see them get hit by Japanese gunfire. That could have been you!

A third bomb hits the *Yorktown*. You feel the heat of the explosion. You head to the bow of the ship and hear a sailor yell, "Submarine!" A torpedo rocks the port side hull. The ship starts to tilt. Then a second torpedo hits below the deck. The ship tilts even more.

Usually, the order to abandon ship would be on the speaker system, but the power is out. Sailors yell, "Prepare to abandon ship!"

You scramble to a lifeboat, thankful to be alive. But you'll always wonder about the sailor you grabbed. He died instead of you. The guilt stays with you until your dying day.

THE END

To follow another path, turn to page 7.
To learn more about the Pacific front, turn to page 103.

CHAPTER 4

BATTLING FOR GUADALCANAL

It's fall 1942. Almost a year has passed since Japan's sudden attack on America at Pearl Harbor. The naval base in Hawaii lost just over 2,400 people. The Japanese also damaged or destroyed 19 American ships.

In June 1942, the U.S. military carried out its own surprise attack at the Battle of Midway in the Pacific Ocean. The Japanese Navy lost four of their six aircraft carriers.

Despite this loss, the Japanese are still fighting for control of the Pacific. The battle is now for Guadalcanal. It's a small island in the Solomon Islands. The Japanese built an airstrip there. If the United States can take it over, they can stop the Japanese from attacking Australia and New Zealand. The code name for the Allies landing in August 1942 is called Operation Watchtower. You are ready to do your part to help the Allied cause.

- To be a Marine medic, called a corpsman, on Guadalcanal, turn to page 74.

- To be the commander of the rescue ship USS *Barton*, turn to page 85.

You're a corpsman with the Marines. The USS *Crescent City* has transported you and other fighters from the United States, Australia, and New Zealand to Guadalcanal. The beach doesn't have docks or catwalks, so the ship takes your regiment to Lunga Point on the north side of the island. It's as close to the beach as possible, but you have to wade through shallow water.

You carry two medical rucksacks. These are all the medial supplies this island will get for awhile. You heave one rucksack on your back and the other on your front. You awkwardly climb over the side of the ship and slide off toward the water. As gravity pulls you down, you fall into the water instead of landing on your feet. You can't get up quickly because of the weight, so you and your supplies get soaked.

Marines charge the beach during the Guadalcanal offensive.

"Whoa, doc, let me help you," a Marine says. He carries one of your dripping rucksacks to the beach.

"Thanks," you tell him.

"No problem," he says. "Call me Roy."

You and Roy head to the beach and drop the rucksacks on the sand.

Turn the page.

The regiment unloads all the supplies and then makes camp deep in the jungle. Everyone is batting away mosquitoes. You were supposed to take first watch, but you ask if you can sort your dry supplies—if there are any. You plan to take a shift tomorrow night. But after chow time, you're called to duty.

Roy has his arm around a Marine, helping him walk. He looks pale and is shivering.

"Howie here just threw up, and he can't remember where he is."

"Malaria," you tell Roy. "His regiment got here a few months ago, so he's been dealing with mosquitoes. I'll get him some quinacrine. It'll help. He can go to the sick bay."

But when you go to your damp rucksacks, the bottles are missing. Where could they have gone?

Would Roy have taken the medicine for himself when he helped you with your rucksack? Do you ask Roy about it and risk being wrong, setting up distrust in your regiment? Or do you not say anything and hope you find the bottles soon? Malaria can kill.

- To ask about the medicine, turn to page 78.
- To hope you find the medicine, turn to page 80.

You decide you cannot mess with malaria. Trust or no trust, you need to ask Roy about the quinacrine bottles. After Howie is settled into his bedding, you pull Roy aside.

"You know when you helped me with my rucksacks?"

Roy nods.

"Did anything fall out?" you ask.

"Not that I know of," he replies.

"Well, I can't find the malaria medicine," you state.

"Let's go to the beach tomorrow and look," Roy says. "I don't want to go through that jungle at night."

You're glad he's not mad. The next morning, you and Roy search the beach.

"Here they are!" You pick up the box, still damp from the day before. "Let's get this to Howie quick."

Not an hour later, you're needed again. One of the Marines checking the camp's perimeter was bit by a crocodile. The croc bit him in the leg, and he's losing a lot of blood. You don't have time to get him to the sick bay. The leg looks bad. You could tie a tourniquet around it to stop the bleeding. Of course, if it's not done right, you may be forced to amputate. The other option is to try to stop the bleeding with pressure instead of a tourniquet and hope to save the leg.

- To use a tourniquet, turn to page 81.
- To apply pressure, turn to page 83.

You decide that asking Roy about the medicine might sound like an accusation. You need to keep looking for the bottles and then ask him about it if you can't find them.

As much as you hate going into the jungle right now, Howie needs that medicine. You grab your flashlight and head toward the beach. The deeper you go, the more nervous you get. Just as you're thinking it was a bad idea to come out here at night, you hear branches breaking. Suddenly, out of the dark shrubs jumps some sort of wild animal. It sinks its teeth into your leg, and you fall to the ground. Your patient isn't going to make it, and now neither will you.

THE END

To follow another path, turn to page 7.
To learn more about the Pacific front, turn to page 103.

This is no place to take chances. You'd rather this Marine lose his leg than his life. You grab a tourniquet out of your rucksack. You tie it off two inches above his knee. You have to be careful with this. If it's too loose, the bleeding won't stop. But if you leave it on too long, it will cause permanent nerve and muscle damage. You may even be forced to amputate.

You want to give the Marine morphine for his pain. But you're afraid it got contaminated when you dropped it in the water. If so, it could kill him.

You sit with your patient for a couple of hours, swatting at the mosquitoes and sweating through your uniform. You check on his leg and see that although the bleeding has slowed, his foot looks very pale. That's not a good sign.

Turn the page.

The next morning, the leg looks the same. The Marine is no longer in shock. He's in a lot of pain. You feel terrible that you can't give him any morphine. If only it hadn't gotten wet. Contaminated medication could kill this man.

You tell Lt. Colonel Puller that the patient needs to be taken off the island to a hospital as soon as possible. Unfortunately, the next transport isn't due for a few weeks. The reality of this dangerous battle finally sinks in. You only hope your side has what it takes to defeat the Japanese.

THE END

To follow another path, turn to page 7.
To learn more about the Pacific front, turn to page 103.

Using a tourniquet can be dangerous. If it it's applied too loosely, the bleeding could get worse. It you take it off too soon, it can damage blood vessels. If it's left on too long, there can be permanent nerve, muscle, and blood vessel damage.

You decide to apply pressure. Luckily, Roy is there to help.

"With both your hands, apply pressure here," you tell him, "We're going to try to stop his bleeding."

You go through your wet supplies and see what you can use. You're afraid the morphine got contaminated in the water. That's the only pain reliever you have. You hope another supply ship brings more.

Turn the page.

You also have sulfa packets to disinfect wounds. They're wet, but you think you can use them under bandages when they dry out. The disinfectant should kill any bacteria. The bandages have to dry out too. You clean and dry your forceps, scissors, and other tools.

You go back to the patient and Roy. "I'll take over," you tell him. The rest of the night, you do what you can to save the Marine's life. But it's not enough. He's gone just as the sun rises. Could using a tourniquet have saved his life? You'll never know.

THE END

To follow another path, turn to page 7.
To learn more about the Pacific front, turn to page 103.

You're in the pilothouse of the destroyer USS *Barton* in the Coral Sea. A radio call comes in from the island of Guadalcanal.

"A plane is down near New Caledonia. Previous rescues have failed. The sea near the island's reef is rough for a rescue. Over."

"Roger that," Clyde, the radio operator, says.

"Can you go in for 17 survivors, plus three pilots? Over," comes the response.

Clyde looks to you for a reply. A few days earlier, you rescued 235 men from the USS *Hornet*, an aircraft carrier attacked by the Japanese. The *Barton* is on its way to drop them off in Brisbane, Australia. But you're still closer to New Caledonia than Australia.

"Affirmative," you say.

Turn the page.

"Roger that," Clyde says. "Give us the last coordinates."

The Japanese may intercept the messages. But it's a risk worth taking to save lives.

You direct the helmsman to steer the *Barton* to the crash site. You get more information as the ship heads northwest of the island of New Caledonia. The C-47 Skytrain was attacked by Japanese forces and got lost. It ran out of fuel and crash-landed on a reef.

An Army plane found the wreck, and an Australian bomber dropped food and blankets. But that was a week after the crash. Three patrol planes tried to rescue the 17 survivors, but they couldn't take off again in the rough water. The survivors and pilots have been stuck in the patrol planes. They're running out of food and growing weaker by the day.

Then you get another message about a possible enemy submarine close by. Maybe you should call in a cruiser to assist you. It's a bigger ship with more room and supplies, and the Japanese will see two ships instead of one. They might be less likely to attack. Of course, waiting for a cruiser means the survivors will have to wait.

the cruiser USS *Denver*

- To call in the cruiser, turn to page 88.
- To continue with the mission, turn to page 93.

You want to attempt the mission now. But there is strength in numbers.

"Call in the *Denver*," you tell Clyde.

The cruiser will be better able to navigate the rough waters. It's also larger and will have more room and supplies for the survivors. Now the question is whether or not to wait here or meet the cruiser farther out to sea. If radar doesn't see any Japanese submarines in the area, it's probably best to stay here. An hour later, you learn that an enemy submarine has been spotted in the area, but it's not showing up on radar yet.

If you stay, you'll be ready to assist with the rescue as soon as the cruiser arrives. But is it worth it to stay where you know a submarine is nearby?

- To stay in the area, go to page 89.
- To leave the area, turn to page 91.

If the submarine isn't showing up on radar, you're probably safe here. You just hope the *Denver* arrives quickly. You go below deck and check on the *Hornet* survivors. Then you hear a sailor calling out.

"Commander! Commander!"

You jump up and run out to meet him.

"The Japanese sub is on radar!" he cries.

You run toward the bridge.

"They weren't there, and then they were," the pale and sweating radar operator explains.

"See if we can get a bomber to protect us," you order.

Clyde starts making requests on the radio.

Not five minutes later, two explosions hit the *Barton*. The sub is attacking you!

Turn the page.

"Radio mayday to any cruisers and destroyers. Let's get everyone on lifeboats," you order Clyde.

But there's not enough time. Another torpedo rocks the ship. You really thought you made the right decision to stay here and wait for the *Denver*. But now that decision cost hundreds of American lives, including yours.

THE END

To follow another path, turn to page 7.
To learn more about the Pacific front, turn to page 103.

There may not be any signs of the Japanese sub on your radar, but knowing it's somewhere close still makes you worry.

"Let's move 50 miles west," you order.

The water is choppy, but the *Barton* slices through it like a hot knife through butter. A few hours later, you're worried that you haven't heard from the *Denver* yet. You request a status from the ship.

Silence.

"Do you think—?" Clyde begins.

"That's what I'm afraid of," you say. The Japanese sunk them. "Let's turn around and stay steady at five knots."

The day ends, and still no call. You decide to head back and attempt the rescue solo.

Turn the page.

All of a sudden, the radio crackles. *"Barton, this is Denver, do you read? Over."*

"Roger, *Denver*," Clyde replies. He looks at you and smiles with relief. "What's your status? Over."

"We came into the vicinity in silence two hours ago because of intelligence reports. We attempted the rescue. It was tough. Rough water with the reef. Sad to report only four were still alive. Over."

Your heart sinks. Leaving cost you critical time. If you had moved sooner, perhaps you could've rescued all 17 survivors, plus the Catalina pilots. You feel like you've failed your country.

THE END

To follow another path, turn to page 7.
To learn more about the Pacific front, turn to page 103.

You can't wait for a cruiser. Those men have been stranded for too long.

You head for New Caledonia. As *Barton* nears the island, you understand what makes this rescue so difficult. The reef near the island makes the waves large and dangerous, and the water is shallow. It's also very windy. There's no way *Barton* can get close.

You have two whaleboats on your ship. These smaller boats can cut through shallow water. The sailors lower them into the water. They take the whaleboats across the waves to one of the planes. You don't see the other two patrol planes and order your lieutenant to find them.

Turn the page.

Meanwhile, the whaleboats struggle to reach the Catalina. The water is too rough. The sailors try to throw a rope to the plane but without success. One sailor jumps in and swims the rope to the plane.

a whaleboat

The first whaleboat then sends a rubber raft to the plane on the rope. The sailor helps load the survivors into the raft. The sailors on the whaleboat pull the raft across the reef and load them into the boat. The sailors take them to the *Barton*. Finally, you can breathe a sigh of relief.

Just then, you receive a report that the other two planes are about three miles from your location. You can get there quickly, but you already have a lot of survivors to deliver to safety. Do you go after the other two planes to rescue the remaining 12 survivors? They've been out at sea for almost two weeks now. Either way, you risk running into the enemy.

- To go after the other two planes, turn to page 96.
- To head to Brisbane, turn to page 101.

You're here now, and those 12 men have been stranded for too long already. You're going to complete this rescue mission.

The ship is just 15 minutes out when two ships are spotted heading your way. It's the Japanese!

If you keep heading toward the patrol planes, you'll risk getting attacked. You'll also lead the Japanese right to the patrol planes. But the longer the survivors have to wait, the greater the chance some won't make it out alive.

You could call for air assistance to attack the ships as you head to the planes. Or you could go the other way and come back tomorrow.

- To call for air assistance, go to page 97.
- To return tomorrow, turn to page 99.

You order Clyde to ask for immediate bomber assistance with a rescue mission. The bombers should distract your enemy while you rescue the survivors.

The *Barton* creeps closer to the drifting patrol planes with no word from any bombers. You can't help but wonder what's taking so long. Fifteen minutes later, still no bombers. You're sweating through your uniform from your nervousness. Suddenly, you hear a voice crackling over the radio.

"*Barton*, this is Lady Betty. Over."

The B-17 bombers have arrived! You don't know how many there are, but it doesn't matter as long as they distract the ships from your rescue mission.

"Roger, Lady Betty," Clyde says.

Turn the page.

"We're approaching the ships. Over," says the voice on the radio. The bombers attack the enemy ships, and you finish your approach to the two patrol planes. Twelve more survivors board your ship. You direct the ship to Brisbane, Australia, where your survivors will finally be safe.

THE END

To follow another path, turn to page 7.
To learn more about the Pacific front, turn to page 103.

You'd be putting everyone on your ship at risk if you continue the rescue now. If you can lay low tonight, the *Barton* can head toward the survivors tomorrow after the enemy is gone.

You turn in the other direction, thinking you're heading toward safety. Suddenly, Clyde shouts, "Submarines, sir!"

"Submarines? More than one?"

the USS *Barton*

Turn the page.

"Afraid so, sir! Two of them are coming at us from behind, and fast."

You direct the boat in the other direction and reach for the speaker system. "MAN BATTLE STATIONS!"

But it's too late, and they're too fast. Their torpedoes hit the hull of the *Barton* one after the other. You won't be rescuing anyone. You and everyone on your ship perishes on the Pacific front.

THE END

To follow another path, turn to page 7.
To learn more about the Pacific front, turn to page 103.

You now have more than 200 survivors on your ship. You're torn but decide to head for Brisbane. These survivors have been through a lot. You want to get them to a safe and well-supplied location soon. You radio the other two patrol planes about another ship heading their way. Then you check your radar. You still don't see any submarines. As your mind shifts to the path ahead, you hear a rumbling in the sky.

"Sir," Clyde says, "our communications must have revealed our location. Enemy bombers are coming in."

You were so worried about submarines, you forgot about the possibility of an air attack.

You look to the sky. To the east, it is thick with enemy planes.

Turn the page.

Alarms blare. Sailors scramble to battle stations. But it's too late. You, your crew, and all of the men you rescued are lost on the Pacific front.

THE END

To follow another path, turn to page 7.
To learn more about the Pacific front, turn to page 103.

CHAPTER 5

THE WORLD AT WAR

World War II began in 1939 when Adolf Hitler led Nazi Germany in an attempt to take over Europe. He wanted support from other countries, and he found it with Italy and Japan. These three countries agreed to help each other if other countries attacked them. Their treaties also declared Italy and Germany as the leaders in Europe and Japan as the leader in Southeast Asia.

The United States did not enter the war right away. But on December 7, 1941, Japan attacked the naval base at Pearl Harbor in Hawaii.

The Japanese Army attacked military airfields, bases, and naval stations with bombs and torpedoes dropped from planes. More than 2,400 U.S. troops died and 1,100 were wounded. Just days later, the United States entered the war on the side of the Allies.

The war had already been raging in Europe. After Pearl Harbor, it surged in the Pacific Ocean too. Two major Pacific battles helped set the course for the United States' ultimate victory.

The Battle of Midway was one of the most important for the U.S. Navy in the Pacific. From June 3 to June 7, 1942, they fought the Japanese in a surprise twist. The Japanese thought they were going to trap the United States' forces, but American code breakers discovered details of the attack. U.S. forces destroyed four aircraft carriers and a cruiser, weakening the Japanese Navy.

Then on August 7, 1942, the United States began its takeover of an airfield on the island of Guadalcanal. After a U.S. win at Guadalcanal, the Japanese could no longer interfere with supply routes to New Zealand and Australia.

Then the Americans and their Allies finished taking over the Pacific one island at a time. The Allied military continued to undermine the Japanese defense. It didn't take long for the Japanese stronghold on the Pacific to disappear.

The Japanese refused to admit defeat. Finally, on August 6, 1945, the United States unleashed the atom bomb. This weapon was more powerful than any the world had ever seen. The U.S. bombed the city of Hiroshima in Japan. Three days later, they bombed Nagasaki. Tens of thousands of people died. This finally forced Japan to surrender.

MAP OF THE PACIFIC FRONT

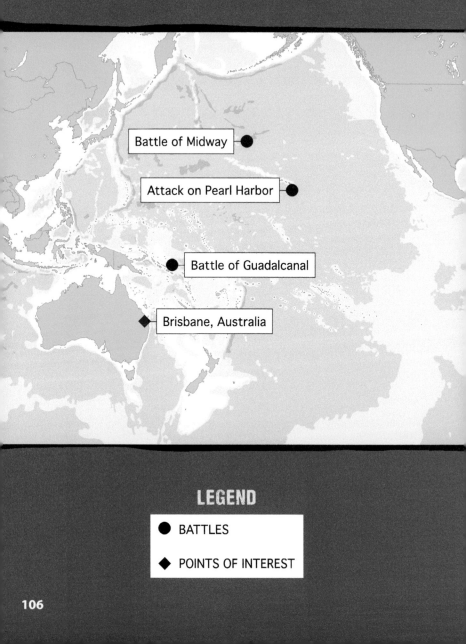

Battle of Midway

Attack on Pearl Harbor

Battle of Guadalcanal

Brisbane, Australia

LEGEND

● BATTLES

◆ POINTS OF INTEREST

TIMELINE

Sept. 1, 1939	Germany invades Poland. World War II begins.
Dec. 7, 1941	Japan attacks Pearl Harbor, Hawaii.
Dec. 8, 1941	U.S. President Franklin Roosevelt asks Congress to declare war against Japan.
Dec. 11, 1941	U.S. Congress declares war against Germany and Italy.
June 3 to June 7, 1942	Code breakers help the U.S. win the Battle of Midway.
Aug. 1942 to Feb. 1943	The U.S. seizes an airstrip on the island of Guadalcanal.
April 1945	Soviet forces surround Berlin in Germany, and Hitler takes his life.
May 7, 1945	Germany surrenders, ending the war in Europe.
Aug. 6 and 9, 1945	U.S. bomber planes drop atomic bombs on the Japanese cities of Hiroshima and Nagasaki.
Aug. 15, 1945	Japan announces surrender.

OTHER PATHS TO EXPLORE

In this book, you've explored several key operations that took place on the Pacific front during World War II. But the experiences of those who served in these situations were just a part of what it was like to live and fight during World War II. How might your perspective change in a different situation?

1. Imagine you were born in Hawaii and are watching the Japanese attack on Pearl Harbor from your home. What can you do as a citizen to help the military after the brutal attack? How do you think this affects your life and culture in the following years?

2. Instead of being in battle on an island or a battleship, imagine you were part of a submarine crew. How would it be living inside a submarine for months? How would battles be different? What ideas, feelings, and fears might you have that would be different than if you were fighting on land?

3. Imagine being one of the survivors waiting for rescue in the Pacific Ocean. How would you survive for more than 10 days? What might you be thinking or feeling?

GLOSSARY

amputate (AM-pyuh-tayt)—to cut off someone's arm, leg, or other body part

critical (KRIT-uh-kuhl)—to be in a dangerous or serious condition

cryptanalyst (krip-tuh-NAL-uh-sist)—a person who interprets secret writings, such as codes or ciphers, when the key is unknown

galley (GAL-ee)—the kitchen area in a ship

malaria (muh-LAIR-ee-uh)—a disease transferred to humans by mosquitoes

shrapnel (SHRAP-nuhl)—bullet shell fragments

tourniquet (TUR-ni-kit)—a medical device for stopping bleeding by compressing a blood vessel, such as using a bandage by twisting

treaty (TREE-tee)—a formal agreement between two or more governments in reference to peace, commerce, or other international relations

verification (vayr-ih-fuh-KAY-shuhn)—proof that something is true

SELECT BIBLIOGRAPHY

Demuth, Patricia. *What Was Pearl Harbor?* New York: Grosset & Dunlap, 2013.

Leckie, Robert. *Challenge for the Pacific: Guadalcanal: The Turning Point of the War.* New York: Bantam Books Trade Paperbacks, 2010 (1965).

Nelson, Craig. *Pearl Harbor: From Infamy to Greatness.* New York: Scribner, 2016.

Symonds, Craig L. *The Battle of Midway.* New York: Oxford University Press, 2011.

"The Pacific Strategy, 1941–1944." The National WWII Museum, New Orleans nationalww2museum.org/war/articles/pacific-strategy-1941-1944

"The Steichen Image: A Portrait of World War II." history.navy.mil/content/history/museums/nmusn/explore/prior-exhibits/1988/steichen-image-portrait-wwii.html#:~:text

READ MORE

Daddis, Susan and Michelle Jovin. *World War II in the Pacific*. Huntington Beach, CA: Teacher Created Materials, 2019.

Doeden, Matt. *What If You Were on the European Front in World War II?: An Interactive Adventure*. North Mankato, MN: Capstone, 2023.

Fowler, Natalie. *A Pearl Harbor Time Capsule: Artifacts of the Surprise Attack on the U.S.* North Mankato, MN: Capstone, 2020.

INTERNET SITES

Pearl Harbor: National Memorial Hawai'i
nps.gov/perl/index.htm

The Battle of Guadalcanal
nationalww2museum.org/war/articles/battle-guadalcanal

World War II in the Pacific: Interactive Timeline
education.nationalgeographic.org/resource/world-war-ii-pacific

ABOUT THE AUTHOR

Lisa M. Bolt Simons has published more than
60 nonfiction children's books, as well as four middle
grade "choose your path" novels and an adult history
book. She's twice received an Honorable Mention
for the McKnight Artist Fellowship for Writers in
Children's Literature. She's also received two Minnesota
State Arts Board grants and other accolades for her
writing. Lisa is a proud mom to her science- and
math-minded twin daughter and son. Originally from
Colorado, Lisa lives in southern Minnesota with her
husband, who also loves to read.